3 Student's Book with Digital Pack

American English

Caroline Nixon & Michael Tomlinson
with Lesley Koustaff & Susan Rivers

T0384661

CAMBRIDGE
UNIVERSITY PRESS

Map of the book

	VOCABULARY	LANGUAGE	SOUNDS AND LETTERS	LITERACY AND VALUES	NUMBERS	CROSS-CURRICULAR	PROJECT
Introduction Page 4							
1 Me! Page 6	Review Level 2: characters, numbers , likes *angry, bored, excited, scared, sleepy, surprised*	*Hello! What's your name? I'm (Kim). How old are you? I'm (eight). I like (books). What's her / his name? She's (Kim). He's (Dan). How old is she / he? She's / He's (eight).* *He's / She's / I'm (bored). He isn't / She isn't / I'm not (bored).*	Review Level 2 letter sounds: *b, m, t, g, p, d, k, n, s, h*	*Jane's name* Be yourself	Review numbers: *1 – 20*	Music: Emotions from music	Make a self portrait
2 My day Page 18	*brush my hair, brush my teeth, get dressed, have breakfast, wake up, wash my face* *go to bed, have dinner, have a snack, listen to a story, play with friends, take a bath*	*I (wake up) (in the morning / every day).* *They / We (play with friends) (after school / in the evening). We / They don't (take a bath).*	Letter sound / ʃ / (sh)	*Brush your hair, Leo!* Take care of yourself	Adding by counting	Social studies: Times of day	Make a daily activities display
3 My home Page 30	*make the bed, pick up the toys, set the table, sweep the floor, wash the clothes, wash the dishes* *bed, bookcase, cabinet, lamp, rug, toy box*	*He / She (washes the dishes). I (sweep the floor).* *It's (under / in / on / next to) the (bed).*	Letter sound /k / (ck)	*Goldilocks and the three bears* Respect other people's things	Numbers: *10, 20, 30, 40*	Social studies: Objects at home	Make and decorate a bedroom
Units 1–3 Review Page 42–43							
4 My sports Page 44	*badminton, baseball, basketball, field hockey, soccer, tennis* *bouncing, catching, hitting, kicking, rolling, throwing*	*They're / She's / He's playing (soccer) .* *She's / He's / They're / I'm (throwing) the ball.*	Letter sound / ŋ / (ng)	*A sport for Grace* Persevere	Subtracting by counting	Physical education: Team sports	Make a ball

	VOCABULARY	LANGUAGE	SOUNDS AND LETTERS	LITERACY AND VALUES	NUMBERS	CROSS-CURRICULAR	PROJECT
⑤ My free time Page 56	*cooking dinner, drawing pictures, listening to music, playing video games, reading books, watching TV* *go roller skating, go swimming, play a board game, play with building blocks, play hide-and-seek, play outside*	*I / We like (reading books).* *Let's (go swimming / play a board game)!* *Can I (come / play)?*	Letter sounds /ʊ/ (short *oo*) and /uː/ (long *oo*)	*Jack loves reading* Join in and help	Numbers: *50, 60*	Art: Paintings, photographs, and sculptures	Make a board game
⑥ My food Page 68	*cake, candy, chips, chocolate, grapes, pineapple* *beans, cereal, fruit, meat, rice, vegetables*	*Would you like some (chocolate)? Yes, please. / No, thank you. I'd like some (candy), please.* *I / We have (meat and rice) for (breakfast / lunch / dinner).*	Letter sound /tʃ/ (ch)	*Share, Ricky Raccoon!* Share	Estimating quantity	Science: Salty, sour, and sweet	Make a plate of food
Units 4–6 Review Page 80–81							
⑦ Animals Page 82	*crocodile, elephant, hippo, monkey, snake, tiger* *duck, giraffe, lizard, parrot, spider, zebra*	*There's (a monkey). There are (three) (monkeys). There are (lots of) (snakes).* *They're (giraffes). They have (long necks / long legs / stripes / short legs / big feet / long tails / sharp teeth). They're (fast).*	Letter sound /θ/ (th)	*The mouse and the lion* Be friendly	Numbers: *70, 80*	Science: Where animals live	Make an animal
⑧ Plants Page 94	*garden, plants, rain, seeds, soil, sun* *beautiful, clean, dirty, new, old, ugly*	*What do plants need? Plants need (sun / rain / soil).* *What (beautiful) (flowers)! What (a dirty) (nose)!*	Letter sound /iː/ (ee, ea)	*Sophia's garden* Work together	Measuring length	Science: How plants grow	Make a plant diagram
⑨ My town Page 106	*hospital, playground, restaurant, school, store, supermarket* *doctor, farmer, nurse, sales clerk, teacher, waiter*	*Where are you / are we going? I'm / We're going to the (supermarket).* *A (teacher) works in a (school). He / She works on a farm. Where does (a teacher) work? Does (a nurse) work (in) a (hospital)? Yes, he / she does. No, he / she doesn't.*	Letter sound /eɪ/ (ay, ai)	*Big-city cat and small-town cat* Appreciate what you have	Numbers: *90, 100*	Social studies: Jobs	Make a jobs poster
Units 7–9 Review Page 118–119							

Hello again!

HOSPITAL

Welcome back to *Pippa and Pop*

1 Me!

 ³ 🎧 **Listen to the song.**

① **Introduction and language review:** *Hello! What's your name? I'm (Kim / Dan / Pippa / Pop / Tinks). How old are you? I'm (eight / five / six / three). I like (books / trains).*

🎧 ⁵ Listen. ⃝ Stick. 📖 Match. 💬 Say.

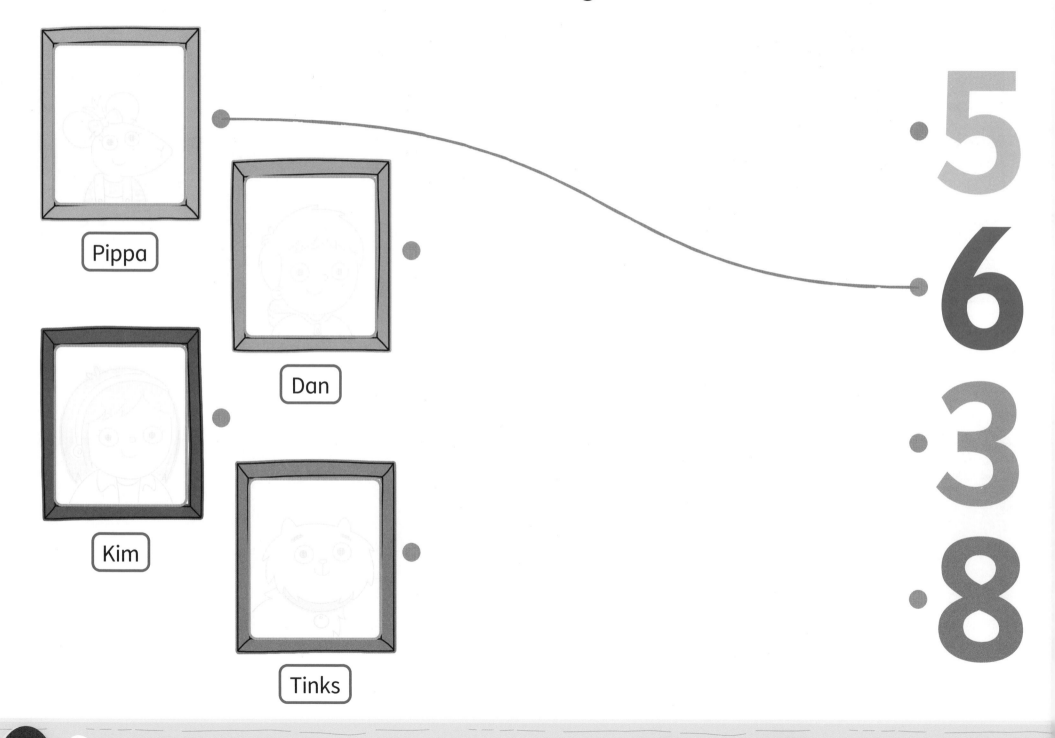

Pippa

Dan

Kim

Tinks

5
6
3
8

1 **Language practice:** *What's your / her / his name? I'm / She's / He's (Kim / Dan / Pippa / Tinks). How old are you / is she / is he? I'm / She's / He's (eight / five / six / three).*

🎧 **⁶ Listen.** ⭕ **Trace.** 📘 **Match.** 💬 **Say.**

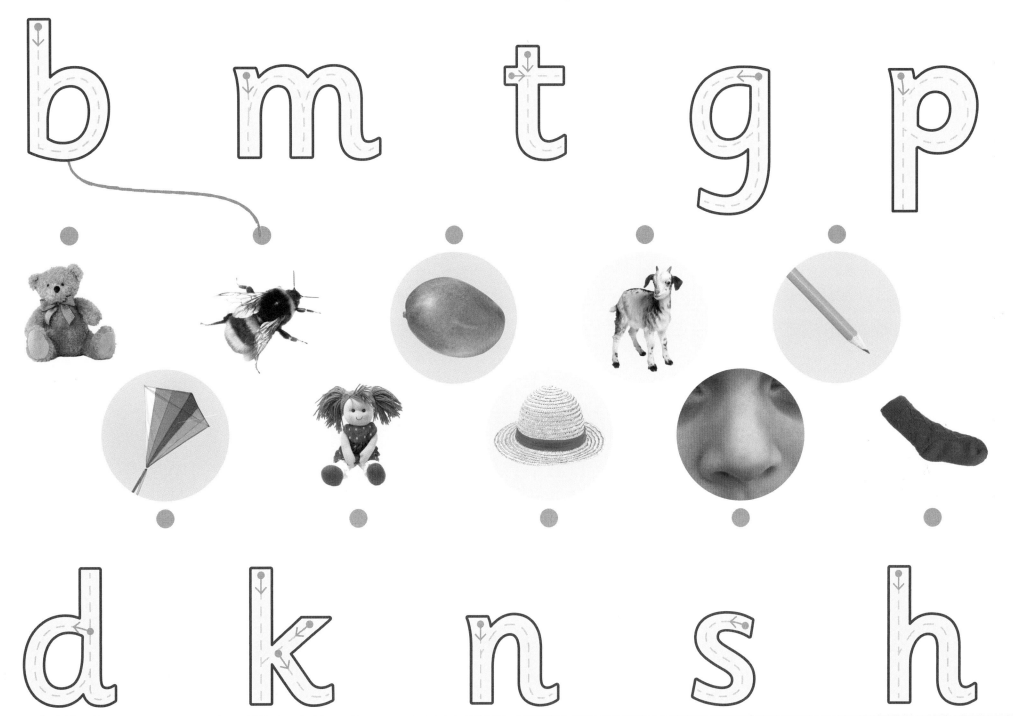

▶ 🎧 (7) Listen. Jane's name

5

I love Jane. She's smart and she's kind.

6

My name isn't Jane.

7

Ahhh, that's nice! Jane is great!

8

Jane is a smart, funny, and kind girl. I'm Jane and I love my name!

▶️ 🎧⁸ Listen. 👆 Point. ⭕ Circle.

Look at Dan. He's bored.

1 **Language presentation:** *He's / She's / I'm (bored / sleepy / surprised / angry / excited / scared). She isn't / He isn't / I'm not (bored).*

bored

angry

excited

scared

surprised

sleepy

Look. Count. Match.

1 2 3 4	**10**	
6 7 8 9	**20**	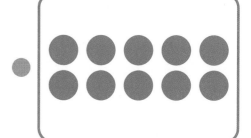
11 12 13 14	**5**	
16 17 18 19	**15**	

🎧 ⁱ⁰ **Listen.** ⭕ **Circle.**

1

2

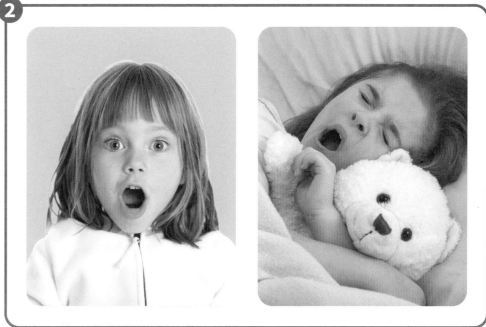

3

4

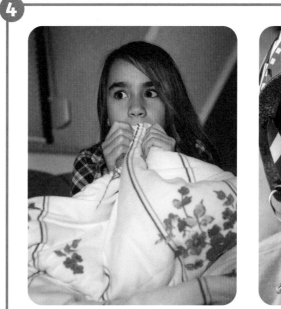 

🎧 Listen. ✏️ Draw. 💬 Say.

1 *He's / She's / I'm (bored / sleepy / surprised / angry / excited / scared). She isn't / He isn't / I'm not (bored).*

◉ Look.   🖐 Make.   💬 Say.

② My day

▶️ 🎧 12 **Listen to the song.**

Let's sing about mornings!

🎧 ⑬ Listen. 👆 Point. ⬭ Trace.

I wake up in the morning.

🎧 ¹⁴ Listen. ➡️➡️ Follow. ◗ Stick. 💬 Say.

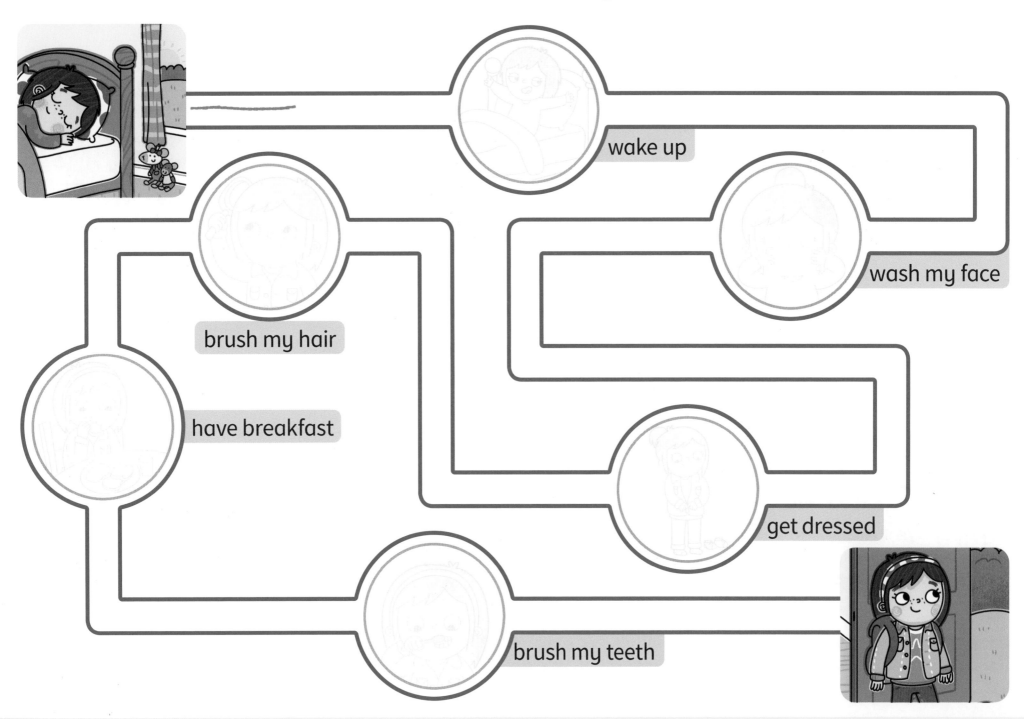

wake up

wash my face

brush my hair

have breakfast

get dressed

brush my teeth

2 **Language practice:** *I (wake up / wash my face / get dressed / brush my hair / have breakfast / brush my teeth) every day.*

🎧 **Listen.** ⭕ **Trace.** ◯ **Circle.** 💬 **Say.**

▶ 🎧 **16 Listen.** **Brush your hair, Leo!**

This is Leo. He's five.

I wake up in the morning.

I put on my jacket.

Bye, Mommy.

Leo, brush your hair!

5

Where's the green boat?

6

Leo can feel something in his hair.

7

I don't like boats in my hair.

8

I wash my face, I brush my teeth, and I brush my hair.

▶ 🎧 (17) **Listen.** 👆 **Point.** ⭕ **Circle.**

1

2 They have a snack after school.

3

4

5

6

2 Language presentation: *They / We (play with friends / have a snack / have dinner / take a bath / listen to a story / go to bed) (after school / in the evening). We don't (take a bath).*

▶️ 🎧 ¹⁸ Listen. ✔️ ✖️ Write a check or an X. 🎵 Sing.

have a snack

play with friends

listen to a story

have dinner

go to bed

take a bath

👋 **Count.** ✏️ **Draw.** ⭕ **Trace.** 💬 **Say.**

$$2 + 1 = 3$$

$$5 + 2 = 7$$

$$6 + 3 = 9$$

$$4 + 4 = 8$$

👁 Look. 📖 Match.

morning

daytime

evening

night

🎧 ¹⁹ Listen. 📖 Match. 💬 Say.

2 *I (wash my face / get dressed / brush my hair / have breakfast / brush my teeth / listen to a story) (in the morning / every day / in the evening).*

👁 Look. 🖐 Make. 💬 Say.

I / We / They (wake up / get dressed / have breakfast / listen to a story / go to bed) in the (morning / evening). I / We / They don't (take a bath) (every day / after school).

③ My home

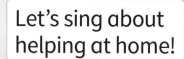

Let's sing about helping at home!

🎧²¹ Listen. 👆 Point. ⭕ Circle.

He washes the dishes.

🎧²² Listen. ⭕ Trace. ⬭ Stick. 💬 Say.

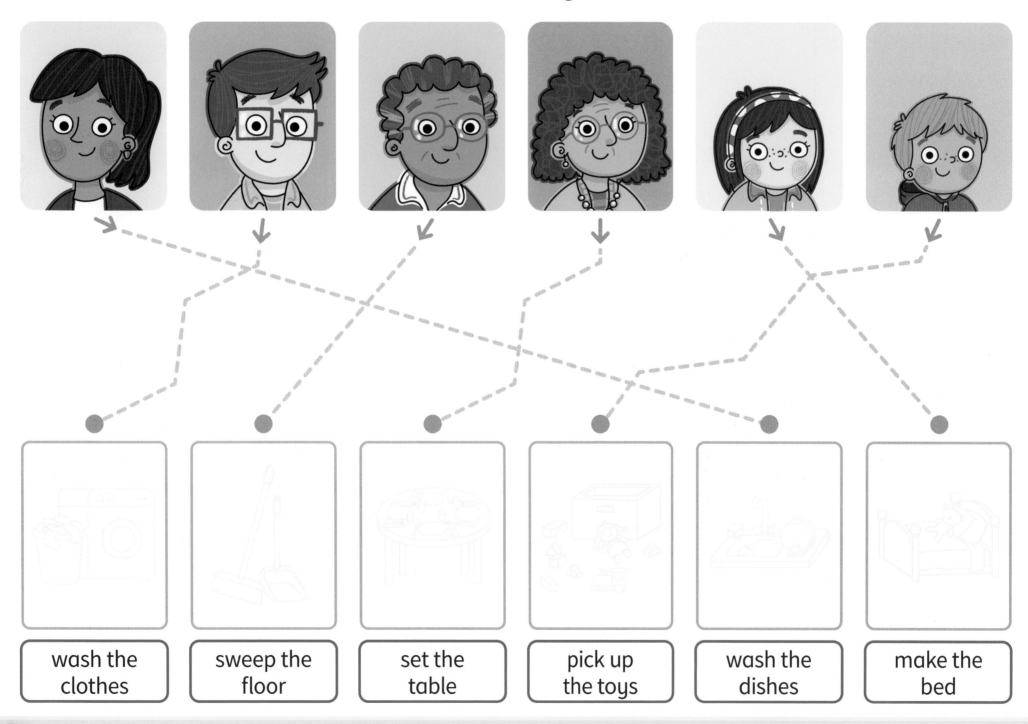

| wash the clothes | sweep the floor | set the table | pick up the toys | wash the dishes | make the bed |

3 Language practice: *He / She (washes the dishes / sets the table / washes the clothes / makes the bed / sweeps the floor). I (pick up the toys).*

Listen. ⬭ Trace. ◯ Circle. 💬 Say.

▶ 🎧(24) Listen. Goldilocks and the three bears

1

> The porridge is very hot. Let's go for a walk.

2 Oh, Goldilocks! It isn't your house!

3 Goldilocks tastes Daddy Bear's porridge.

4 Goldilocks tastes Baby Bear's porridge.

5 Goldilocks sits on Baby Bear's chair.

6 Goldilocks tries Baby Bear's bed.

7

Where's my porridge? Look at my chair!

8

I'm very sorry. I can make the beds.

3 Language presentation: *It's (under / on / in / next to) the (bed / rug / cabinet / toy box / lamp / bookcase).*

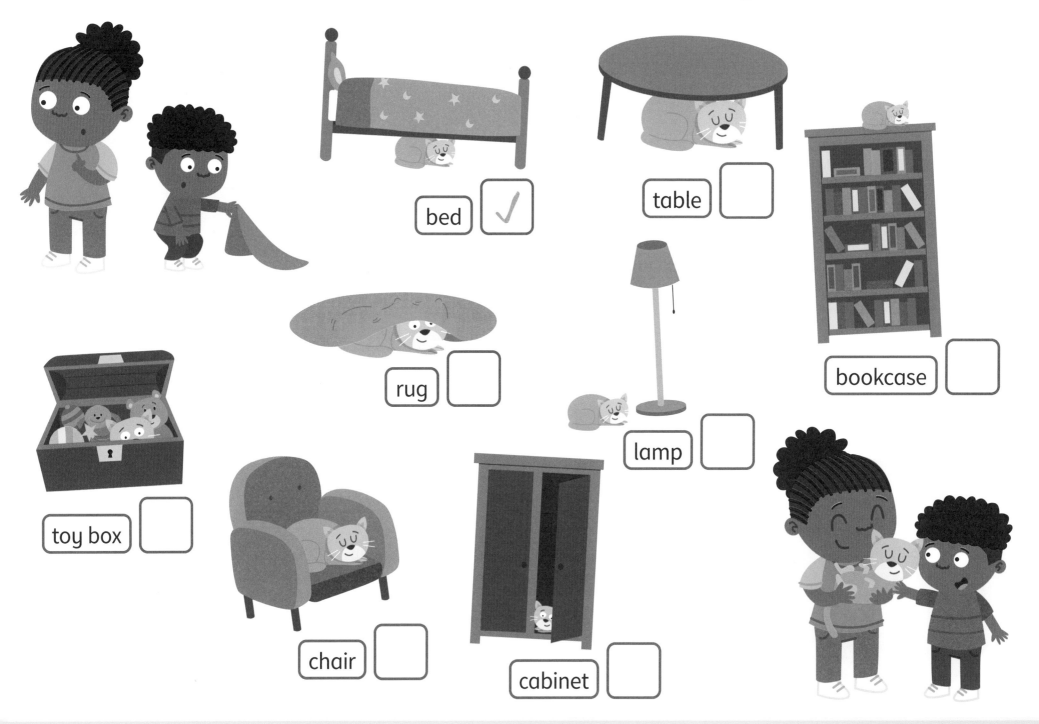

▶ 🎧 ²⁶ **Listen.** ✔ ✘ **Write a check or an X.** 🎵 **Sing.**

bed ✔

table

bookcase

rug

toy box

lamp

chair

cabinet

🎧 **Listen.** ⭕ **Trace.** ✋ **Count.** ✏️ **Color.**

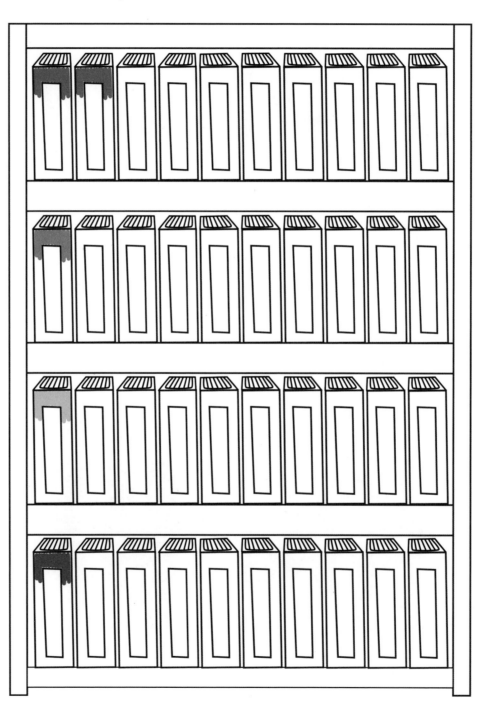

👁 Look. 📖 Match.

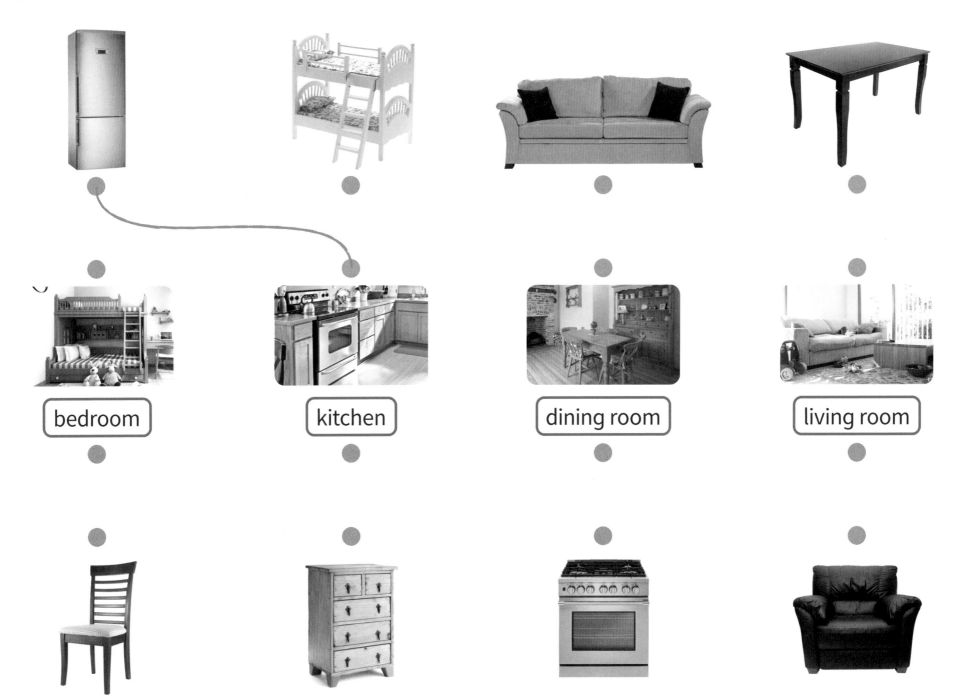

bedroom

kitchen

dining room

living room

🎧 Listen. 📖 Match. 💬 Say.

3 *He / She (washes the dishes / picks up the toys / sets the table / washes the clothes / makes the beds / sweeps the floor) (in the morning).*

👁 Look. 🖐 Make. 💬 Say.

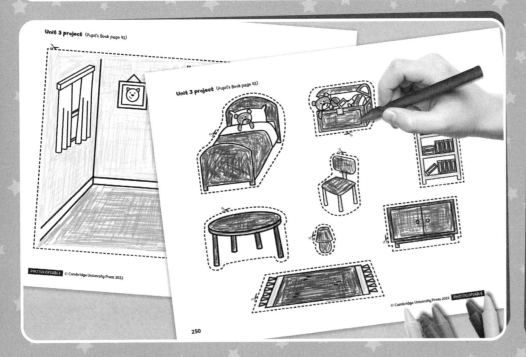

🎧 **29 Listen.** 🔍 **Find.** 🔢 **Number.** 💬 **Say.**

✋ Count. ✏️ Draw. ✏️ Write.

$4 + 2 = \underline{6}$

$5 + 3 = \underline{}$

$10 + 1 = \underline{}$

$10 + 10 = \underline{}$

(4) My sports

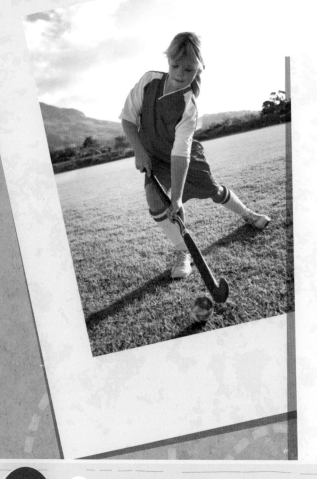

Let's sing about sports!

🎧 ³¹ Listen. ☝ Point. 1²3 Number.

They're playing soccer.

1

Listen. Trace. Stick. Say.

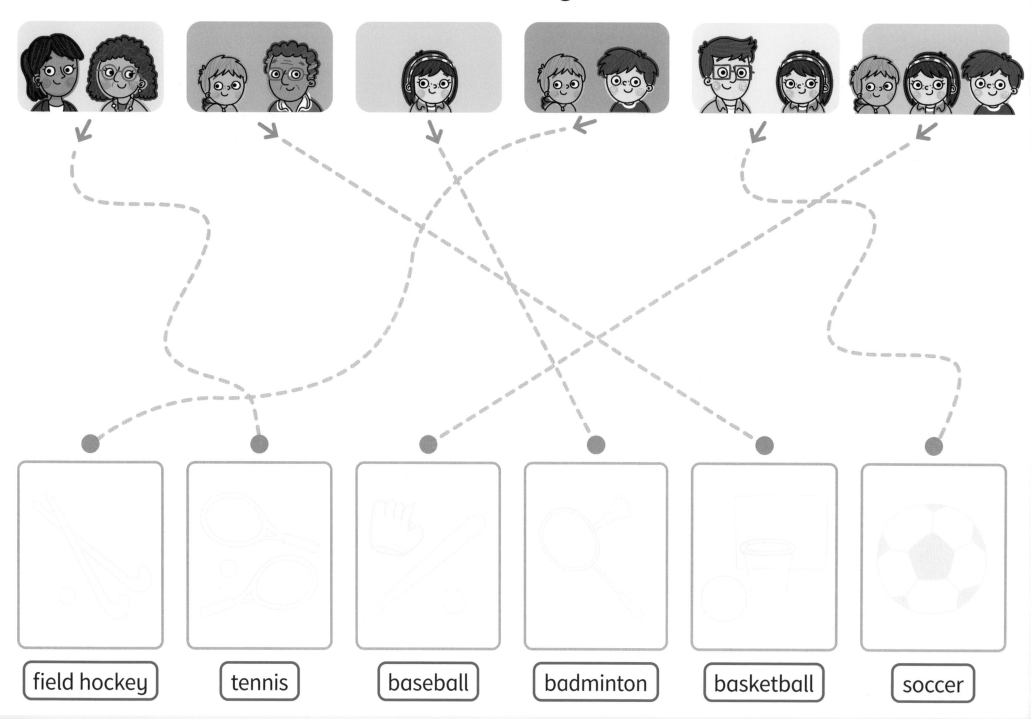

| field hockey | tennis | baseball | badminton | basketball | soccer |

4 **Language practice:** *They're / She's / He's playing (soccer / badminton / tennis / baseball / field hockey / basketball).*

🎧 ³³ **Listen.** ◌ **Trace.** ◯ **Circle.** 🗨 **Say.**

1

2

3

4

🎬 🎧 ³⁵ Listen. 👆 Point. ⭕ Circle.

1

She's throwing the ball.

2

3

4

5

6

4 **Language presentation:** *She's / He's / They're / I'm (throwing / hitting / catching / bouncing / rolling / kicking) the ball.*

 **Listen.** 👁 **Look.** ○ **Circle.** 🎵 **Sing.**

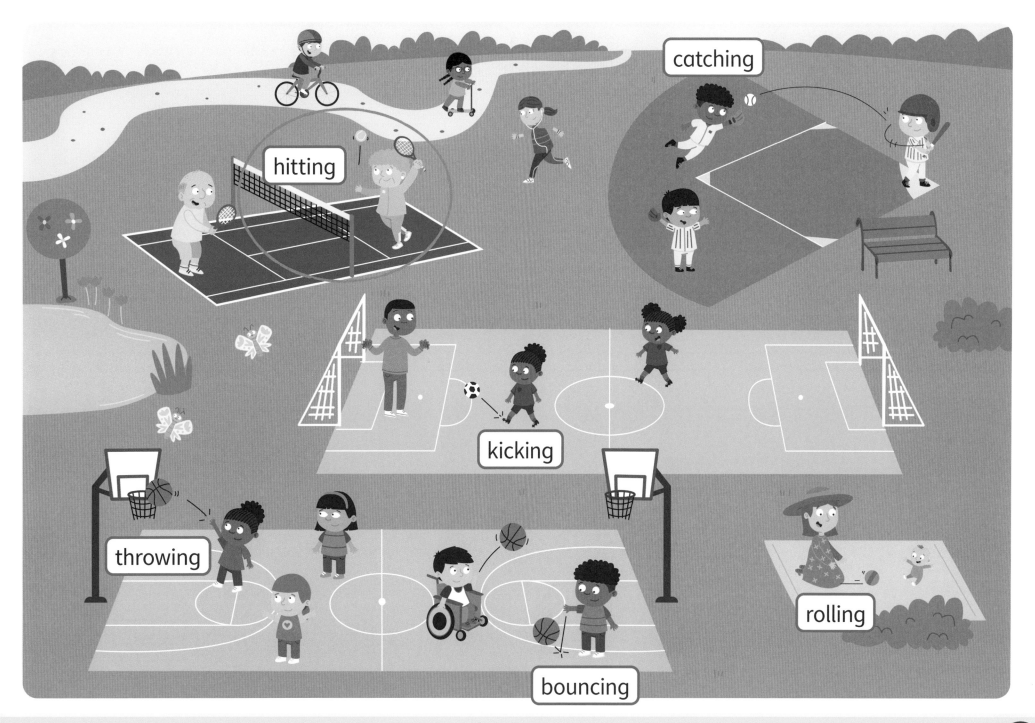

catching

hitting

kicking

throwing

bouncing

rolling

✋ **Count.** ✏️ **Draw.** ⭕ **Trace.** 🟦 **Say.**

$$3 - 2 = 1$$

$$6 - 1 = 5$$

$$7 - 4 = 3$$

$$10 - 8 = 2$$

🎧37 **Listen.** 📖 **Match.**

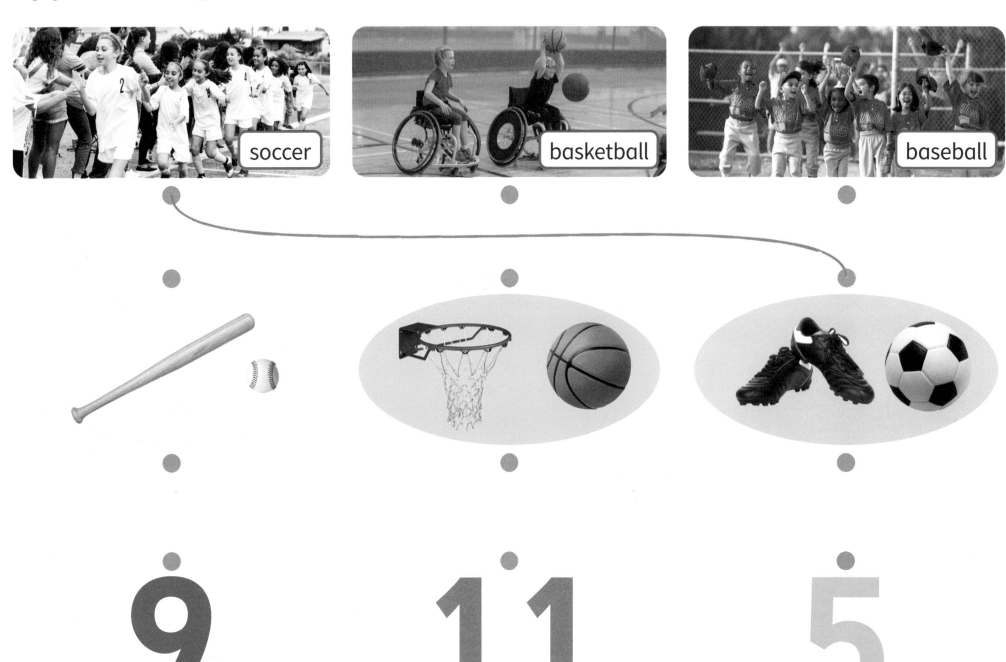

soccer

basketball

baseball

9

11

5

Review

🎧 **38 Listen.** ✔ ✘ **Write a check or an X.** 💬 **Say.**

1
 ✔

2

3

4

5

6

7

8

4 *They're / She's / He's playing (soccer / badminton / tennis / baseball / field hockey / basketball). They're / She's / He's (throwing / hitting / catching / bouncing / rolling / kicking) the ball.*

👁 Look. 🖐 Make. 😊 Play.

⑤ My free time

 🎧 39 **Listen to the song.**

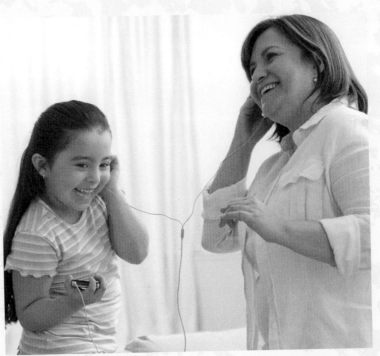

Let's sing about having fun!

🎧⁴⁰ Listen. ☝ Point. 1²³ Number.

🎧⁴¹ Listen. ⭕ Trace. 🔵 Stick. 🟦 Say.

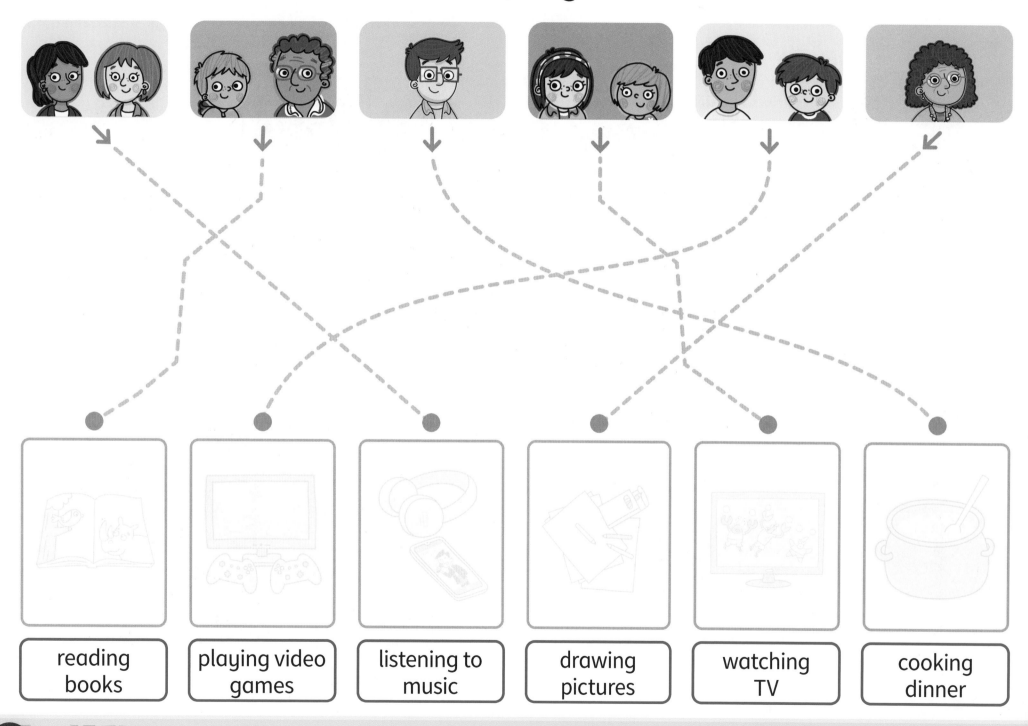

reading books

playing video games

listening to music

drawing pictures

watching TV

cooking dinner

5 Language practice: *I / We like (reading books / cooking dinner / watching TV / playing video games / listening to music / drawing pictures).*

🎧⁴² **Listen.** ⬭ **Trace.** ◯ **Circle.** 🔲 **Say.**

▶ 🎧43 Listen. Jack loves reading

1

Jack likes reading books.

2

Jack likes superheroes.

3

Jack, come and help, please.

4

Jack, please set the table.

Come and help, please, Jack!

Jack's mommy isn't happy.

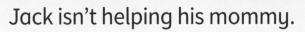

Jack isn't helping his mommy.

Superheroes help. I can help, too.

1

2

3

4

5

6

5 **Language presentation:** *Let's (go swimming / go roller skating / play a board game / play with building blocks / play outside / play hide-and-seek)! Can I (come / play)?*

▶️ 🎧 **Listen.** ✔️ ❌ **Write a check or an X.** 🎵 **Sing.**

go roller skating

play outside

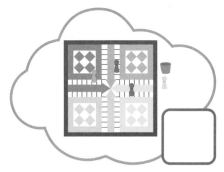
play a board game

play tennis

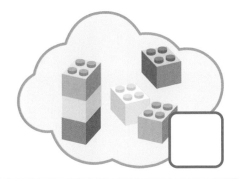
play with building blocks

go swimming

play soccer

play hide-and-seek

Language practice: *Let's (go swimming / go roller skating / play a board game / play with building blocks / play outside / play hide-and-seek)! Can I (come / play)?* 5

🎧 **⁴⁶ Listen.** ◯ **Trace.** ✋ **Count.** ▯ **Match.**

10 20 30 40 50 60

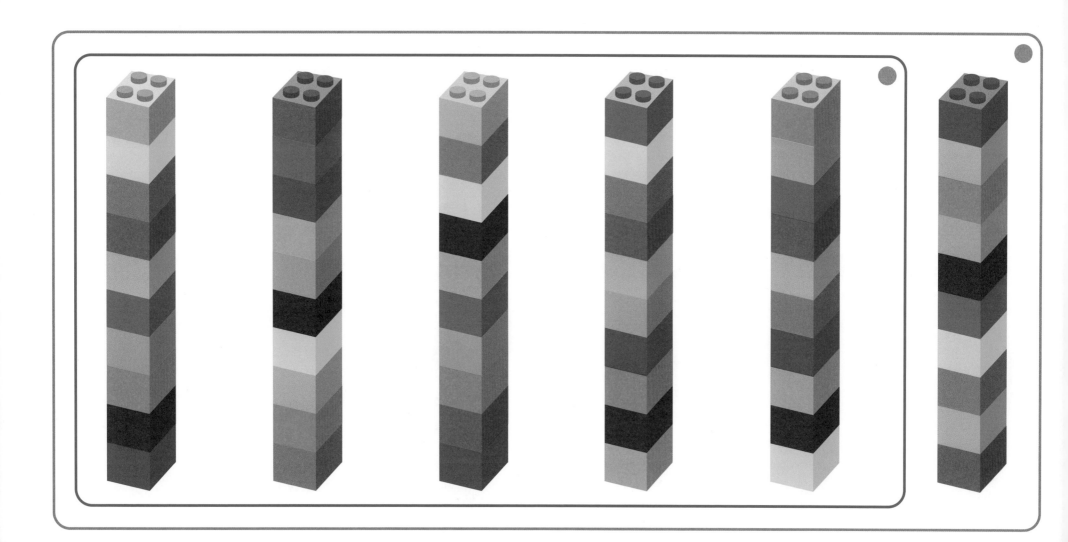

👁 Look. 📖 Match.

painting

photograph

sculpture

🎧 Listen. 1̶2̶3̶ Number. 💬 Say.

1

5 *I / We like (reading books / cooking dinner / watching TV / playing video games / listening to music / drawing pictures).*

👁 Look. 🖐 Make. 😊 Play.

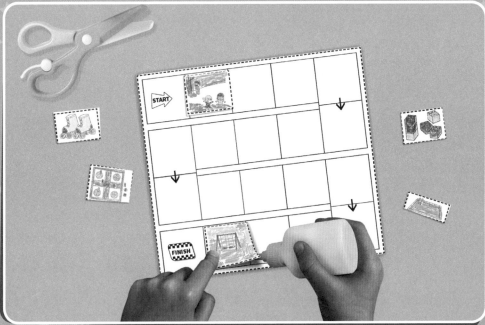

⑥ My food

Let's sing about food!

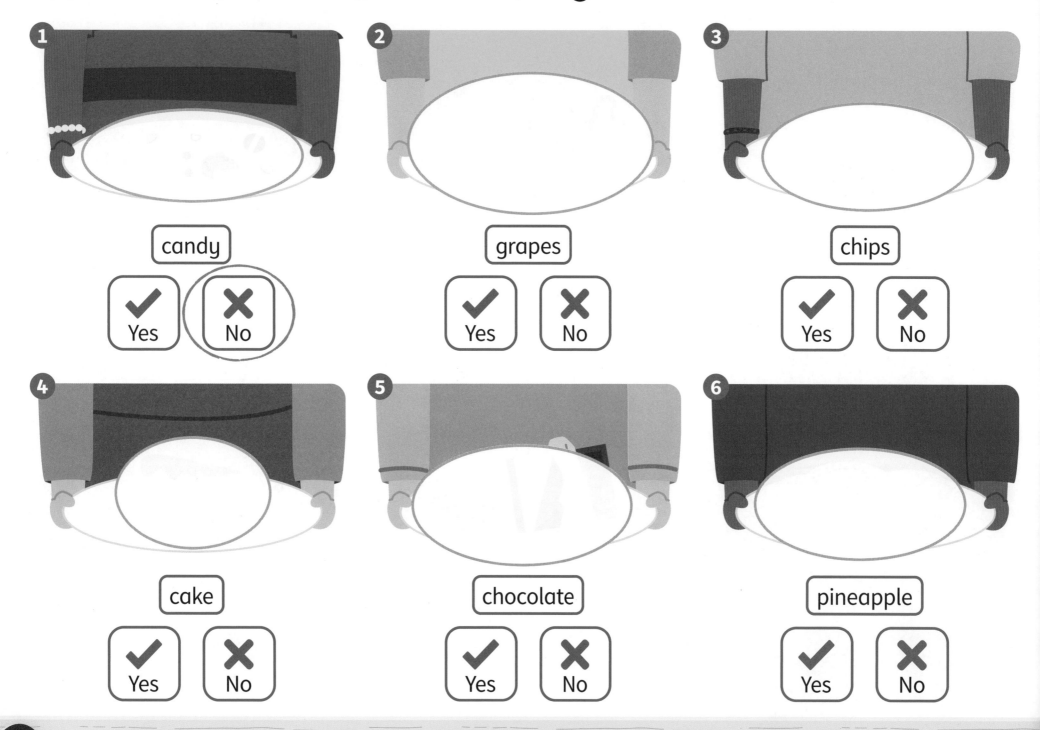

Listen. Stick. Circle. Say.

1 candy — ✔ Yes / ✘ No

2 grapes — ✔ Yes / ✘ No

3 chips — ✔ Yes / ✘ No

4 cake — ✔ Yes / ✘ No

5 chocolate — ✔ Yes / ✘ No

6 pineapple — ✔ Yes / ✘ No

6 Language practice: *Would you like some (chocolate / grapes / chips / candy / pineapple / cake)? Yes, please. / No, thank you.*

🎧 ⁵¹ **Listen.** ⭕ **Trace.** ✏️ **Color.** 💬 **Say.**

Share, Ricky Raccoon!

1

Ricky is eating the candy.

2

Ricky is eating the ice cream.

3

Where's our ice cream?

4

Ricky is eating the cake.

Ricky is sharing!

2 We have fruit and cereal for breakfast.

6 Language presentation: *I / We have (meat / rice / fruit / cereal / vegetables / beans) for (breakfast / lunch / dinner).*

▶️ 🎧 54 Listen. ✔️❌ Write a check or an X. 🎵 Sing.

bread and fruit ✔️

bread and eggs

meat and rice

vegetables and rice

meat and beans

rice and beans

sandwiches and milk

cereal and milk

■ **Say.** ○ **Circle.** ✋ **Count.** ✏ **Write.**

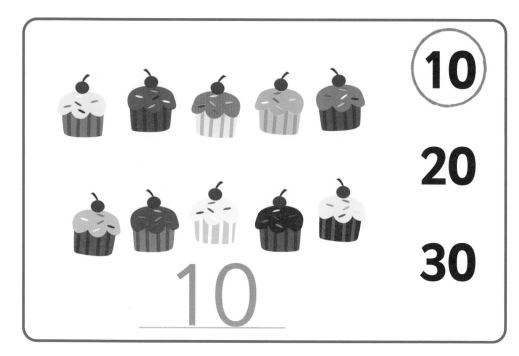

（**10**）

20

30

10

20

40

60

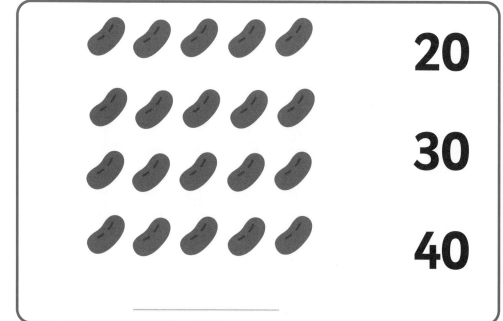

20

30

40

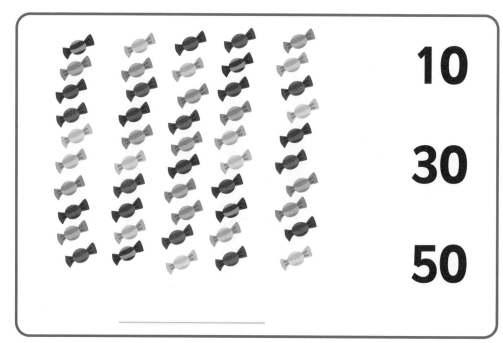

10

30

50

◉ Look. ○ Circle.

salty

sour

sweet

Review

🎧 **55** Listen. 📖 Match. 💬 Say.

6 *Would you like some (chocolate / grapes / chips / candy / pineapple / cake)? Yes, please. / No, thank you. I'd like (lots of) grapes.*

👁 Look. 🖐 Make. 💬 Say.

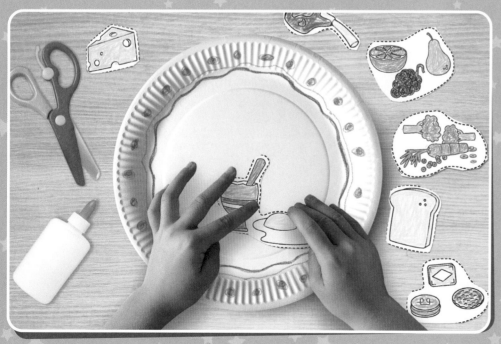

👋 Count. ✏️ Draw. 🖊️ Write.

$$6 - 3 = 3$$

$$8 - 2 = \underline{\hspace{2cm}}$$

$$10 - 7 = \underline{\hspace{2cm}}$$

$$9 - 5 = \underline{\hspace{2cm}}$$

7 Animals

Let's sing about animals!

🎧⁵⁸ Listen. 👆 Point. 🔢 Number.

There are two elephants.

There's a tiger.

59 Listen. Stick. Match. Say.

tigers | crocodile | elephants

1 1 2 3 4 7

hippos | monkeys | snake

7 **Language practice:** *There's (a crocodile / a snake). There are (two) (tigers / monkeys / hippos / elephants). There are lots of (monkeys).*

🎧⁶⁰ **Listen.** ⭕ **Trace.** ⭕ **Circle.** 💬 **Say.**

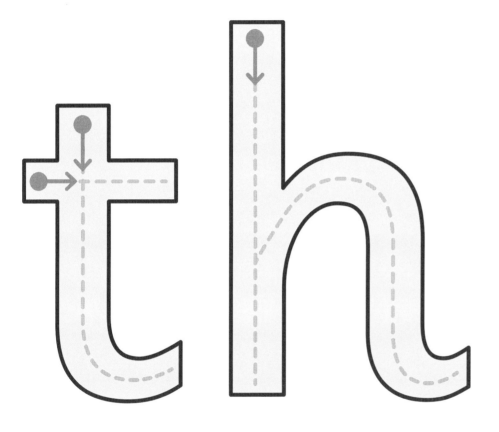

▶ 🎧61 Listen. The mouse and the lion

The mouse sees a big lion.

You're very big and I'm very small.

I'm small, but I'm not scared.

The lion wakes up!

▶ 🎧 62 Listen. 👆 Point. ⭕ Circle.

They have long necks. They're tall.

7 **Language presentation:** *They're (giraffes / zebras / ducks / parrots / lizards / spiders). They have (long necks / long legs / stripes / short legs / big feet / long tails). They're (fast).*

▶ 🎧 **63 Listen.** ⬭ **Trace.** ✏️ **Color.** 🎵 **Sing.**

giraffes

zebras

parrots

ducks

spiders

lizards

🎧 **64** **Listen.** ⭕ **Trace.** ✋ **Count.** ✏️ **Color.**

10 20 30 40 50 60 70 80

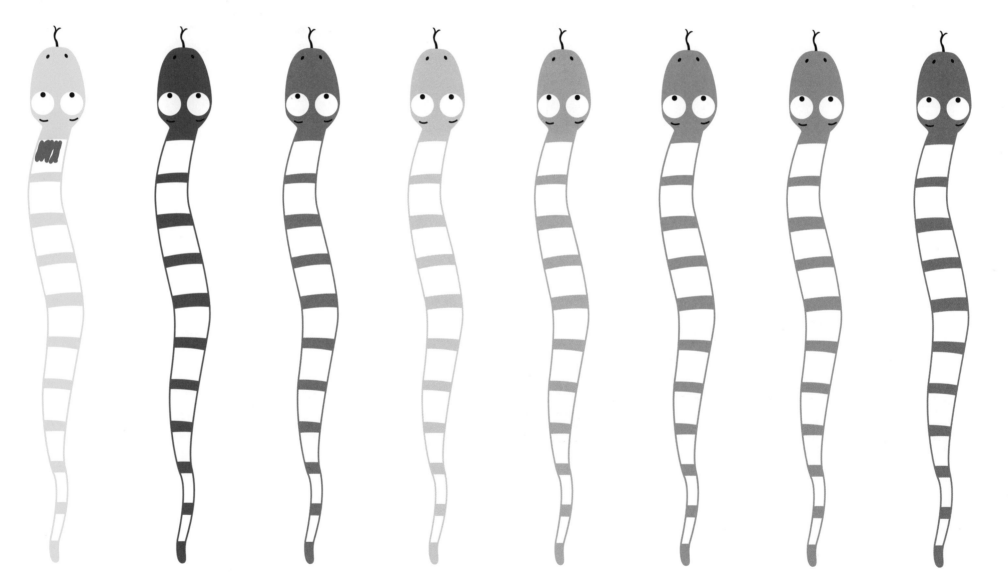

🎧 **Listen.** 👁 **Look.** 📘 **Match.**

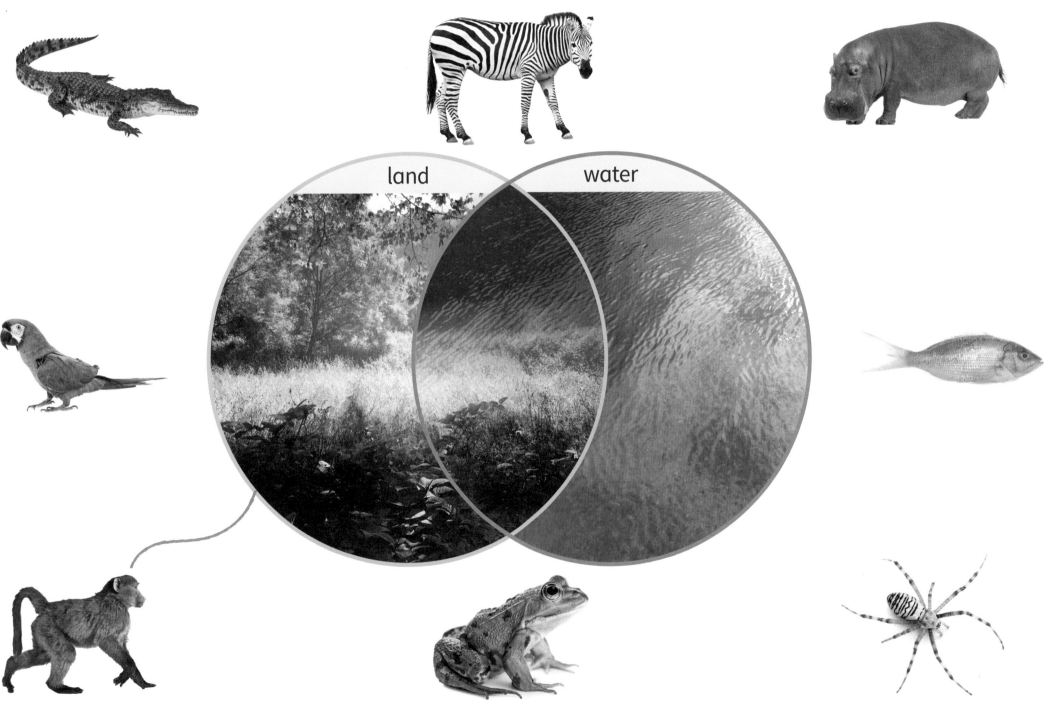

land   water

🎧 ⁶⁶ Listen. ⭕ Circle. 💬 Say.

1

parrots

lizards

2

zebras

hippos

3

ducks

crocodiles

4

giraffes

elephants

7 *They're (giraffes / zebras / ducks / parrots / lizards / crocodiles / hippos / elephants). They have (long necks / long legs / stripes / short legs / long tails / sharp teeth / small ears).*

👁 Look. 🤚 Make. 💬 Say.

There's a (tiger / snake / spider). There are (four) (tigers). There are (lots of) (snakes). **7** 93

(8) Plants

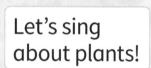

Let's sing about plants!

🎧 ⁶⁸ Listen. 👆 Point. 🔢 Number.

Plants need rain.

1

🎧⁶⁹ Listen. ◯ Stick. 💬 Say.

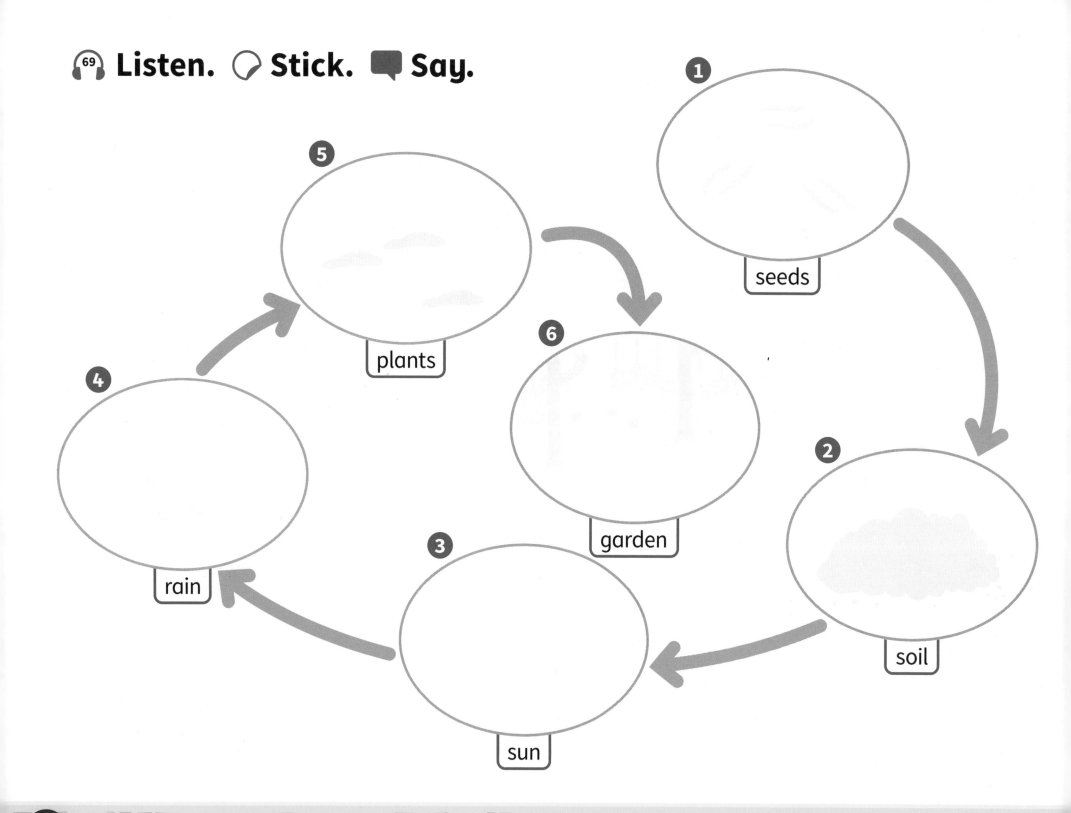

1 seeds

2 soil

3 sun

4 rain

5 plants

6 garden

8 Language practice: *garden, seeds, plants, sun, rain, soil; Plants need (sun / rain / soil).*

🎧 70 **Listen.** ⬭ **Trace.** ◯ **Circle.** 🔲 **Say.**

▶ 🎧 71 Listen. Sophia's garden

1

Sophia wants a garden.

2

The sun and the rain cloud are watching.

3

It rains and rains. The plants can't grow.

4

Plants need sun.

5

The plants can't grow. Plants need rain.

6

Sophia is sad.

7

The sun and the rain cloud work together.

8

What a beautiful garden!

▶️ 🎧 ⁷³ Listen. ✔️ ✖️ Write a check or an X. 🎵 Sing.

beautiful ✔️

ugly

beautiful

dirty

new

new

old

dirty

clean

👁 **Look.** ✋ **Count.** ✏ **Write.**

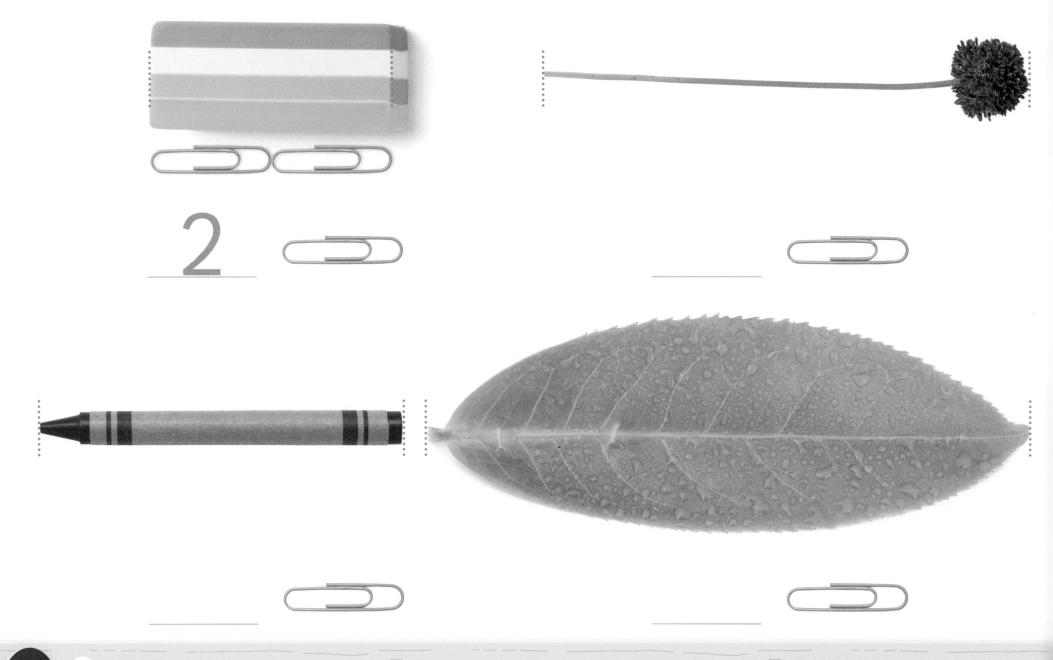

2

👁 Look. 1̶2̶3̶ Number.

Review

8 *beautiful, dirty, ugly, new, old, clean; What (dirty) (hands)! What (an ugly) (beach)!*

👁 Look. 🖐 Make. 💬 Say.

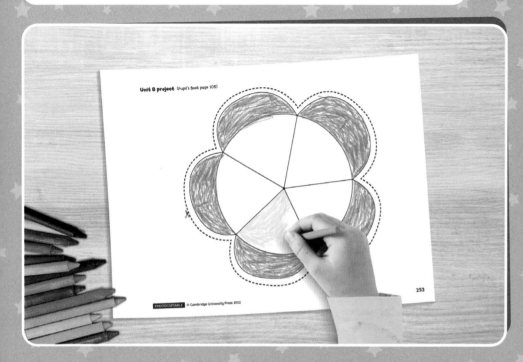

Plants need sun.

⑨ My town

Let's sing about going to town!

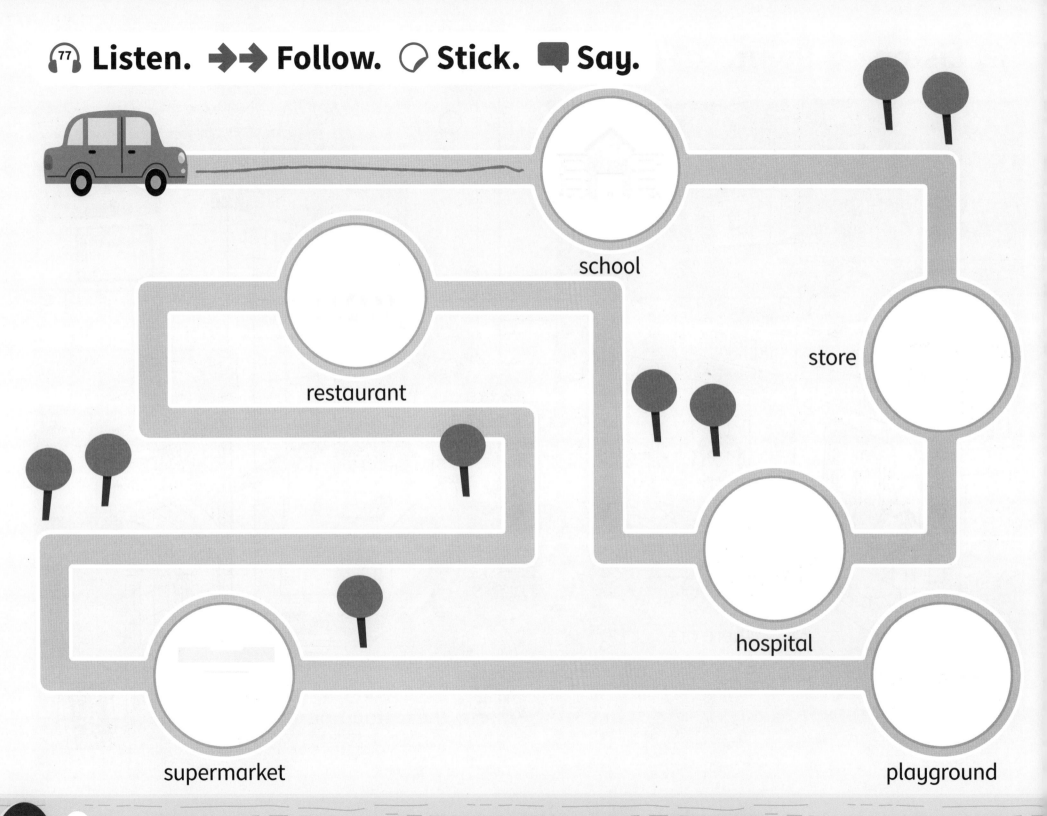

school

restaurant

store

supermarket

hospital

playground

🎧 **78 Listen.** ⭕ **Trace.** ◯ **Circle.** 🔲 **Say.**

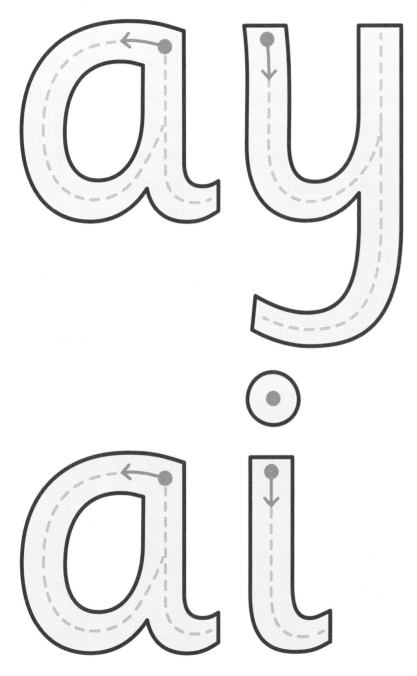

▶ 🎧 79 **Listen.** **Big-city cat and small-town cat**

5

Welcome to my small town, Bill.

It's very quiet.

6

Bill and Ben are tired.

It's dirty!

7

I don't like the small town.

CITY

8

Ben and Bill say goodbye.

1

2

3

4

5

6

▶️ 🎧 ⁸¹ Listen. 📖 Match. 🎵 Sing.

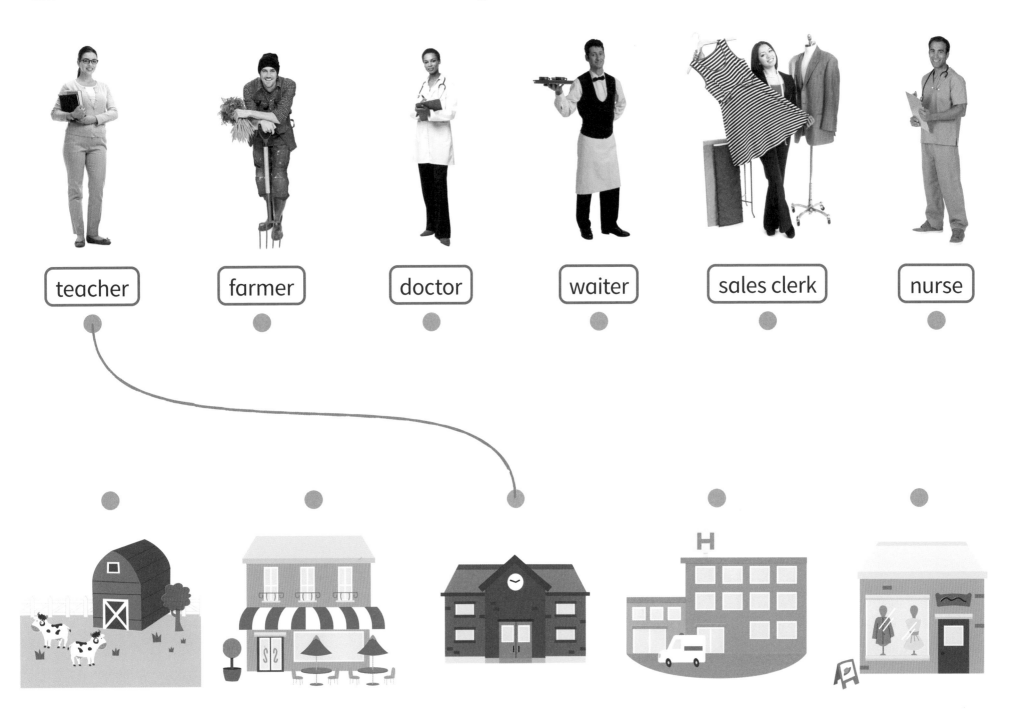

teacher   farmer   doctor   waiter   sales clerk   nurse

🎧 **82** **Listen.** ⭕ **Trace.** ✋ **Count.** ✏️ **Color.**

20 **40** **60** **80** **100**

10 **30** **50** **70** **90**

🎧 83 Listen. 👁 Look. ✔✖ Write a check or an X.

1

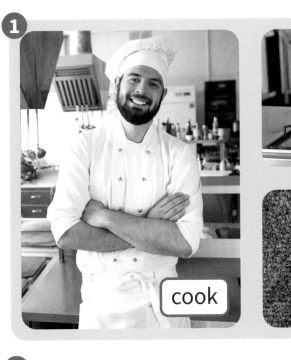

cook

 ✔

2

dentist

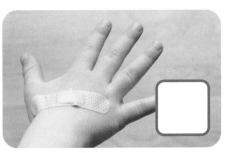

3

farmer

4

bus driver

🎧 (84) Listen. 🔍 Find. 123 Number. 💬 Say.

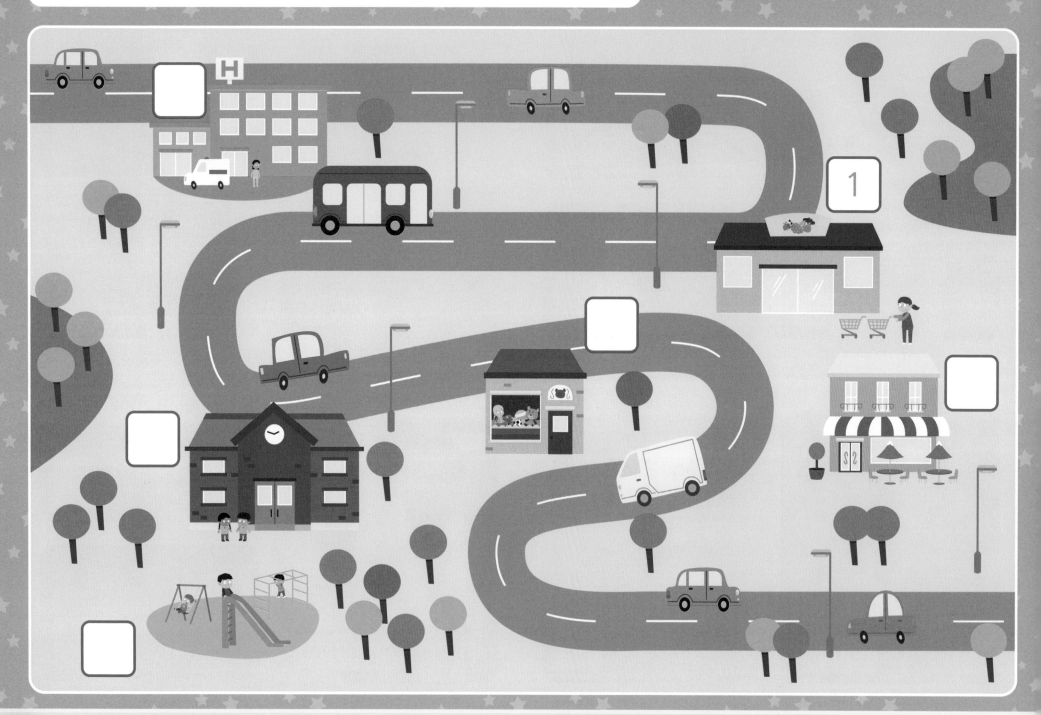

9 *Where are we going? We're going to the (supermarket / restaurant / hospital / store / school / playground).*

👁 Look. 🖐 Make. 💬 Say.

Unit 9 project (Pupil's Book page 117)

A cook works in a restaurant.

🎧 85 **Listen.** 🔍 **Find.** 123 **Number.** 💬 **Say.**

Look. Count. Circle.

20 🌱 40 🌷 60 100 🌰

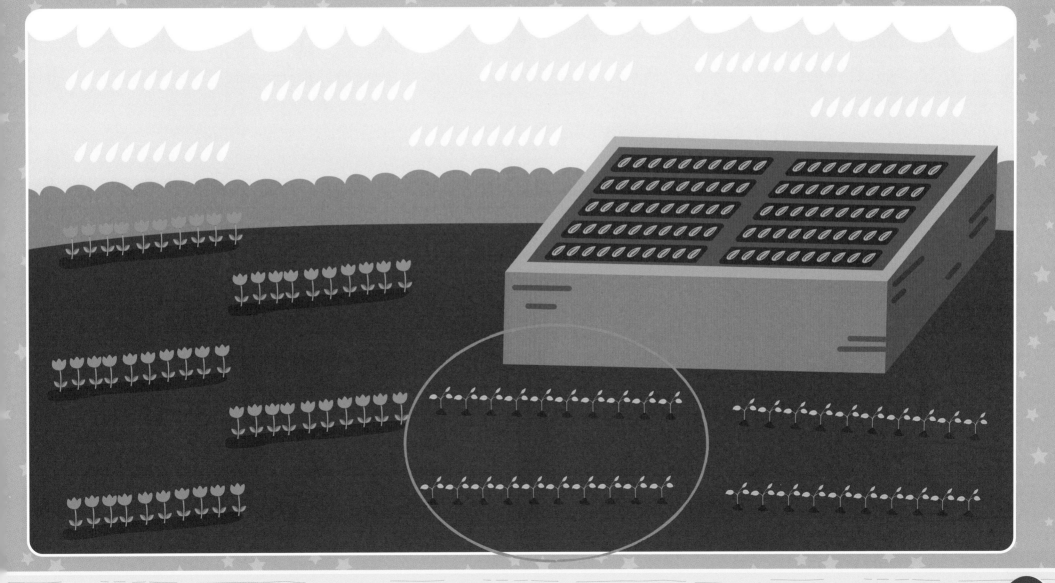

Thanks and Acknowledgements

Authors' thanks

Many thanks to everyone at Cambridge University Press for their dedication and hard work in extraordinarily complicated circumstances, and in particular to:

Liane Grainger for her unwavering professionalism and her irrepressible joviality;

Emily Hird for her endless enthusiasm, good humor, and sound judgment;

Jane Holt for her unflagging energy and her ability to bring the whole, sprawling project together;

Vanessa Gold for her hard work and sound editorial contribution.

Catherine Ball and Carolyn Wright for their hard work helping to review, correct, and knead the manuscript into shape.

Our thoughts and hearts go out to all the teachers and their students who have suffered and continue to suffer the devastating effects of the global pandemic that has changed all our lives. Stay strong.

Dedications

For Giuseppe Vincenti with love. The biggest and strongest heart I know. – CN

For Paloma, Pablo, and Carlota, keep on smiling, love – MT

Caroline Nixon and Michael Tomlinson, Murcia, Spain

The publishers and authors would like to thank the following contributors:

Additional writing by Lesley Koustaff, Susan Rivers, and Catherine Ball.

Book design and page make-up by Blooberry Design.

Cover design by Blooberry Design.

Commissioned photography by Blooberry Design.

Freelance editing by Catherine Ball, Karen Cleveland Marwick, Amy Griggs, and Carolyn Wright.

Editorial project management by Emma Ramírez.

Audio recording and production by Leon Chambers.

Original songs and chants by Robert Lee.

Songs and chants production by Jake Carter.

Animation production by QBS and Collaborate Agency.

The authors and publishers acknowledge the following sources of copyright material and are grateful for the permissions granted. While every effort has been made, it has not always been possible to identify the sources of all the material used, or to trace all copyright holders. If any omissions are brought to our notice, we will be happy to include the appropriate acknowledgements on reprinting and in the next update to the digital edition, as applicable.

Key: U = Unit.

Photography

All photos are sourced from Getty Images.

U1: Mike Kemp; FatCamera/E+; photosindia; Blurra/E+; Antagain/E+; Richard Newstead/Moment; FRANCOIS-EDMOND/iStock/Getty Images Plus; GlobalP/iStock/Getty Images Plus; kali9/E+; ElementalImaging/iStock/Getty Images Plus; PhotoAlto/Laurence Mouton/PhotoAlto Agency RF Collections; zayatssv/iStock/Getty Images Plus; Roland Magnusson/EyeEm; Nirut Punshiri/EyeEm; Jose Luis Pelaez Inc/Digital Vision; Imgorthand/E+; Lea Paterson/Science Photo Library; Caroline Schiff; Juanmonino/istock/Getty Images Plus; Westend 61; Ideabug/istock/Getty Images Plus; Asya_mix/iStock/Getty Images Plus; Lubushka/iStock/Getty Images Plus; Mai Vu/iStock/Getty Images Plus; antadi1332/iStock/Getty Images Plus; Irina_Strelnikova/iStock/Getty Images Plus; **U2:** JohnyGreig/E+; Kelvin Murray/Photodisc; ER productions limited/Digital vision; Corbis/VCG; Tetra Images; Damircudic/E+; Khilagan/iStock/Getty Images Plus; Sally Anascombe/Stone; PhotoNotebook/iStock/Getty Images Plus; JGI/Jamie Grill; Chris Hackett; Jose A. Bernat Bacete/Moment; Jiri V'aclavek/EyeEm; Kyoshino/iStock/Getty Images Plus; Westend 61; Sean Locke/Photodisc; Jose Luis Pelaez Inc/Digital Vision; Deyangeorgiev/iStock/Getty Images Plus; Solstock/iStock/Getty Images Plus; Zubbin Shroof/The Image bank; Ariel Skelley/Digital Vision; Monkeybuisnessimages/iStock/Getty Images Plus; Image Source; eurobanks/iStock/Getty Images Plus; Elinamaninen/iStock/Getty Images Plus; Secret agent mike/moment; Serezniy/iStock/Getty Images Plus; Pictofoloia/E+; Asya_mix/iStock/Getty Images Plus; Lubushka/iStock/Getty Images Plus; Mai Vu/iStock/Getty Images Plus; BRIAN MITCHELL/Corbis Documentary; SDI Productions/E+; antadi1332/iStock/Getty Images Plus; Irina_Strelnikova/iStock/Getty Images Plus; **U3:** Imagenavi; Ned Frisk; Uwe krejci/DigitalVision; Explora_2005/iStock/Getty Images Plus; Juzant/Digital vision; John Keeble/Moment; Mint Images RF; Grenme/iStock/Getty Images Plus; Ednam/iStock/Getty Images Plus; JazzIRT/E+; Creatikon Studio/iStock/Getty Images Plus; Atiati/E+; YangYin/E+; Skrow/E+; Luminis/iStock/Getty Images Plus; Siri Stafford/Digital Vision; Westend 61; Bonnie Tarpey - Wronski/EyeEM; Bobbieo/iStock/Getty Images Plus; Gabe Palmer/The Image Bank; Antagain/E+; Kevin trimmer/Moment; Peter Dazeley/The Image Bank; Brizmaker/iStock/Getty Images Plus; Martin Poole/The Image bank; Carolyn Hebbard/Moment Open; Asya_mix/iStock/Getty Images Plus; Lubushka/iStock/Getty Images Plus; Mai Vu/iStock/Getty Images Plus; antadi1332/iStock/Getty Images Plus; Irina_Strelnikova/iStock/Getty Images Plus; **U4:** FatCamera/E+; SwellMedia/UppercutImages; PeopleImages/E+; ThomasBarwick/DigitalVision; ArielSkelley/DigitalVision; Amstockphoto/iStock/GettyImagesPlus; JillFormer/Photographer'schoiceRF; PongnatheeKluaythong/EyeEm; CSquaredStudios/Photodisc; Barcin/iStock/GettyImagesPlus; KinzieRiehm/ImageSource; PeterTitmuss/UniversalImagesGroup; DennisLane; SamEdwards/OJOImages; emholk/E+; HMVart/E+; TimClayton-Corbis; Asya_mix/iStock/Getty Images Plus; Lubushka/iStock/Getty Images Plus; Mai Vu/iStock/Getty Images Plus; antadi1332/iStock/Getty Images Plus; Kohei Hara/DigitalVision; Irina_Strelnikova/iStock/Getty Images Plus; **U5:** ViewStock; BraunS/E+; JoseLuisPelaezInc/DigitalVision; Fuse/Corbis; lisegagne/E+; MarkDouet/TheImageBank; Cirilopoeta/E+; thenakedsnail/Moment; CaseyHillPhoto/E+; Tomekbudujedomek/Moment; RichardT.Nowitz/TheImageBank; oxygen/Moment; MassimoPizzotti/Photographer's Choice RF; AlexanderSorokopud/Moment; TimHall/Cultura; LittleBee80/iStock/GettyImagesPlus; Westend61; Prostock-Studio/iStock/GettyImagesPlus; Hiroshi Higuchi/The Image Bank; AleksandarNakic/E+; Asya_mix/iStock/Getty Images Plus; Lubushka/iStock/Getty Images Plus; Mai Vu/iStock/Getty Images Plus; antadi1332/iStock/Getty Images Plus; MsMoloko/iStock/Getty Images Plus; **U6:** Image Source; NWphotoguy/E+; Wavebreakmedia; Foodcollection; Peter Dazeley/Photodisc; artisteer/iStock/Getty Images Plus; Brian Macdonald/DigitalVision; HandmadePictures/iStock/Getty Images Plus; bombuscreative/iStock/Getty Images Plus; margouillatphotos/iStock/Getty Images Plus; Rani Sr Prasiththi/EyeEm; Matt Walford/Cultura; Lisa Barnes/Moment; The Picture Pantry/Alloy; ViewStock; FGorgun/iStock/Getty Images Plus; gangnavigator/iStock/Getty Images Plus; Petra Matjasic/EyeEm; Tetra Images; Zen Rial/Moment; Bloxsome Photography/Moment; byryo/iStock/Getty Images Plus; Asya_mix/iStock/Getty Images Plus; Lubushka/iStock/Getty Images Plus; Mai Vu/iStock/Getty Images Plus; antadi1332/iStock/Getty Images Plus; Irina_Strelnikova/iStock/Getty Images Plus; **U7:** Peter Unger/Stone; Vicki Jauron, Babylon and Beyond Photography/Moment; Mike Hill/Stone; Tatsiana Volskaya/Moment; Vera Buerkle/EyeEm; avi11/E+; Theo Allofs/Stockbyte; Nneka Mckay/EyeEm; Peter Groenendijk/robertharding; Aditya Singh; kuritafsheen/RooM; Brand X Pictures/Photodisc; Mikel Cornejo/EyeEm; Xuanyu Han/Moment; vusta/E+; DaddyBit/iStock/Getty Images Plus; GlobalP/iStock/Getty Images Plus; Brian Hagiwara/The Image Bank; Martin Harvey/The Image Bank; George Doyle & Ciaran Griffin/Stockbyte; Yuxin Xiao/500px; Eve Livesey/Moment; SG Wildlife Photography/500px; StuPorts/iStock/Getty Images Plus; Vivian Yeong/EyeEm; Manoj Shah/Photodisc; Manoj Shah/Stone; Sir Francis Canker Photography/Moment; Asya_mix/iStock/Getty Images Plus; Lubushka/iStock/Getty Images Plus; Mai Vu/iStock/Getty Images Plus; antadi1332/iStock/Getty Images Plus; Simon Phelps Photography/Moment; Irina_Strelnikova/iStock/Getty Images Plus; **U8:** Neumann & Rodtmann/The Image Bank; sarayut Thaneerat/Moment; Eskay Lim/EyeEm; temmuzcan/iStock/Getty Images Plus; Paula French/EyeEm; mikroman6/Moment; temmuzcan/E+; Studio Light and Shade/iStock/Getty Images Plus; taketan/Moment; Westend61; Liliboas/E+; Richard Sharrocks/Moment; AtlasStudio/iStock/Getty Images Plus; ihorga/iStock/Getty Images Plus; EHStock/iStock/Getty Images Plus; akepong/iStock/Getty Images Plus; Richard Clark/The Image Bank; Libby Hipkins/Moment; Yanuar Sudrajat/EyeEm; ClarkandCompany/iStock/Getty Images Plus; Tetsuya Tanooka/Aflo; Rachel Weill/UpperCut Images; Stefan Cristian Cioata/Moment; Kate Kunz/Corbis; Freer Law/iStock/Getty Images Plus; Matteo Colombo/Moment; tunart/E+; Ohmega1982/iStock/Getty Images Plus; Rolfo Brenner/EyeEm; Gail Shotlander/Moment; docksnflipflops/iStock/Getty Images Plus; Kameleon007/iStock/Getty Images Plus; FotografiaBasica/E+; Asya_mix/iStock/Getty Images Plus; Lubushka/iStock/Getty Images Plus; Nicolae Gherasim/EyeEm; Mai Vu/iStock/Getty Images Plus; antadi1332/iStock/Getty Images Plus; Irina_Strelnikova/iStock/Getty Images Plus; **U9:** Bruno De Hogues/Stockbyte; Morsa Images/DigitalVision; Ariel Skelley/DigitalVision; stoonn/iStock/Getty Images Plus; SCI_InDy/iStock/Getty Images Plus; Dina Alfasi/EyeEm; Sally Anascombe/DigitalVision; levente bodo/Moment; Mint Images/Mint Images RF; Andrew Peacock/Stone; Ljupco/iStock/Getty Images Plus; Fridholm, Jakob; londoneye/iStock/Getty Images Plus; C Squared Studios/Photodisc; YinYang/iStock/Getty Images Plus; 4x6/E+; mediaphotos/E+; stockvisual/iStock/Getty Images Plus; amstockphoto/iStock/Getty Images Plus; Tetra Images/Brand X Pictures; AnthonyRosenberg/iStock/Getty Images Plus; Fuse/Corbis; Ariel Skelley/DigitalVision; Vlad Fishman/Moment; Asya_mix/iStock/Getty Images Plus; Lubushka/iStock/Getty Images Plus; Mai Vu/iStock/Getty Images Plus; Irina_Strelnikova/iStock/Getty Images Plus; Hispanolistic/E+ antadi1332/iStock/Getty Images Plus; SDI Productions/E+; Maskot; Aaron Foster/DigitalVision.

Illustrations

Amy Zhing; Beatriz Castro; Begoña Corbalán; Dean Gray; Louise Forshaw, and Collaborate Agency artists.

Cover illustration by Collaborate Agency.

1 Me! (Page 8)

2 My day (Page 20)

3 My home (Page 32)

4 My sports (Page 46)

5 My free time (Page 58)

6 My food (Page 70)

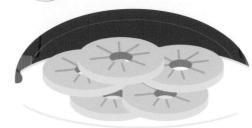 

6 My food (Page 70)

7 Animals (Page 84)

8 Plants (Page 96)

9 My town (Page 108)